Manners on the Telephone

by **Carrie Finn**   illustrated by **Chris Lensch**

PICTURE WINDOW BOOKS
Minneapolis, Minnesota

Special thanks to our advisers for their expertise:

Kay Augustine, Associate Director
Institute for Character Development at Drake University

Susan Kesselring, M.A., Literacy Educator
Rosemount–Apple Valley–Eagan (Minnesota) School District

Editor: Nick Healy
Designer: Tracy Davies
Page Production: Melissa Kes
Art Director: Nathan Gassman
Associate Managing Editor: Christianne Jones
The illustrations in this book were created digitally.

Picture Window Books
151 Good Counsel Drive
P.O. Box 669
Mankato, MN 56002-0669
877-845-8392
www.picturewindowbooks.com

Printed in China.
102009
005543

Library of Congress Cataloging-in-Publication Data
Finn, Carrie.
Manners on the telephone / by Carrie Finn ; illustrated
by Chris Lensch.
p. cm. – (Way to be!)
Includes bibliographical references and index.
ISBN-13: 978-1-4048-3156-8 (library binding)
ISBN-13: 978-1-4048-3561-0 (paperback)
ISBN-13: 978-1-4048-5996-8 (paperback)
1. Telephone etiquette–Juvenile literature. 2. Etiquette
for children and teenagers–Juvenile literature. I. Lensch,
Chris. II. Title.
BJ2195.F56 2007
395.5'9–dc22   2006027568

Using the telephone to call friends or family can be fun. Phone calls can also be very useful in everyday life. Everyone wants to talk without any problems. Good manners on the phone help make that happen.

There are lots of ways you can use good telephone manners.

When he answers the phone, Kyle says, "Hello, this is the Jackson residence."

He is using good manners.

Naomi speaks in a clear voice on the phone. She does not yell or whisper.

She is using good manners.

Lydia answers the phone, but the call is for her brother. She says, "Just a minute, please. I'll get David for you."

She is using good manners.

Alexis does not yell her brother's name when the call is for him. She goes to find him.

She is using good manners.

Cameron answers a call for his mother. He gently sets down the phone and goes to get her.

He is using good manners.

Bryce says, "Sorry, my mom can't come to the phone right now." He does not tell the caller that his mom is in the bathtub.

He is using good manners.

14

Gretchen is polite when the caller has the wrong number. She says, "Sorry, you dialed the wrong number."

She is using good manners.

Colby needs to talk to Justin, but Justin's mom answers the call. Colby says, "Hello, this is Colby. May I please speak with Justin?"

He is using good manners.

Joanna says "Goodbye and thanks for calling" before hanging up the phone.

She is using good manners.

The telephone is an important tool for many people. Good manners can make the telephone work for you. You can talk to friends and family, and you can be sure you will be heard.

Fun Facts

People with good manners turn off their cell phones in restaurants and movie theaters.

The first cordless phone was invented in 1965 by a woman named Teri Pall.

American inventor Alexander Graham Bell's first words spoken into the telephone were "Mr. Watson, come here. I want to see you."

In England, telephone booths are bright red.

When using a cell phone in public, you should lower your voice and keep calls short to avoid disturbing others.

The first international phone call made through an underwater cable was from London to Paris in 1891.

To Learn More

At the Library

Ashley, Susan. *I Can Use the Telephone.* Milwaukee: Weekly Reader Early Learning Library, 2005.

DeGezelle, Terri. *Manners on the Telephone.* Mankato, Minn.: Capstone Press, 2004.

Elerding, Louise. *You've Got Social Manners! Party Pointers from A to Z.* Burbank, Calif.: Grandy Publications, 2004.

On the Web

FactHound offers a safe, fun way to find Web sites related to this book.
All of the sites on FactHound have been researched by our staff.

1. Visit *www.facthound.com*

2. Type in this special code: 1404831568

3. Click on the FETCH IT button.

Your trusty FactHound will fetch the best sites for you!

Index

Look for all of the books in the Way to Be! series:

Being a Good Citizen: A Book About Citizenship

Being Fair: A Book About Fairness

Being Respectful: A Book About Respectfulness

Being Responsible: A Book About Responsibility

Being Trustworthy: A Book About Trustworthiness

Caring: A Book About Caring

Manners at School

Manners at the Table

Manners in Public

Manners in the Library

Manners on the Playground

Manners on the Telephone